MAKE UNIQUE

A Sletchbook of Creative Housing Designs

Ron Lokkesmoe

"This world is but a canvas to our imagination."

Henry David Thoreau

MAKE UNIQUE
Copyright 2014 - Ron Lokkesmoe

For information please contact the author at:
RonLokk@gmail.com

FIRST EDITION
Printed in the United States of America

ISBN-10: 1500763764

ISBN-13: 978-1500763763

INTRODUCTION

This collection of hand drawn sketches is being presented for everyone who would like to build or remodel a home. The design concepts in this sketchbook were inspired by homes created by various designers, along with several homes that Ron designed and built all by himself. For those who appreciate the organic qualities of freehand drawings, you won't want to miss this collection of unique housing designs.

When it comes to being unique, you might think that every conceivable shape has already been utilized. Or, you might be under the impression that the only way to be unique is to create something that looks absurd. That is why it is so valuable to collaborate with an experienced designer, who can offer refreshing ideas to make your home pleasurable to live in and incredibly beautiful to look at.

In addition to shape, a good design concept must consider many other critical factors to take full advantage of its location. Is there a spectacular view that you will not want to miss? Will you require easy access for a wheelchair? Do you prefer privacy, or would you like your home to be close to the road? Can the sun provide heat, or a tree give cool shade? These are just a few of the factors for you to consider.

Since it is ideal to live in harmony with nature, it is also important to determine the impact that your home will have on the environment. It is also beneficial to consider how the environment will impact your living space, which is what the Native Americans did when they built their dwellings in the Mesa Verde cliffs almost 1,000 years ago. For whether you live in a Tiny House or a McMansion, it is worthwhile to build a home that works well with the landscape.

In general, designing a home is like creating an intricate puzzle, and it is up to you to determine the overall theme and where the various parts will go. From selecting the right size and location to determining the most essential features for your home, you can make choices that best meet your needs. The end result is that you will have a home that you can enjoy and be proud of!

DEDICATION

I dedicate this book to my wife,

Barbara,

who helped in so many ways to make this book possible.

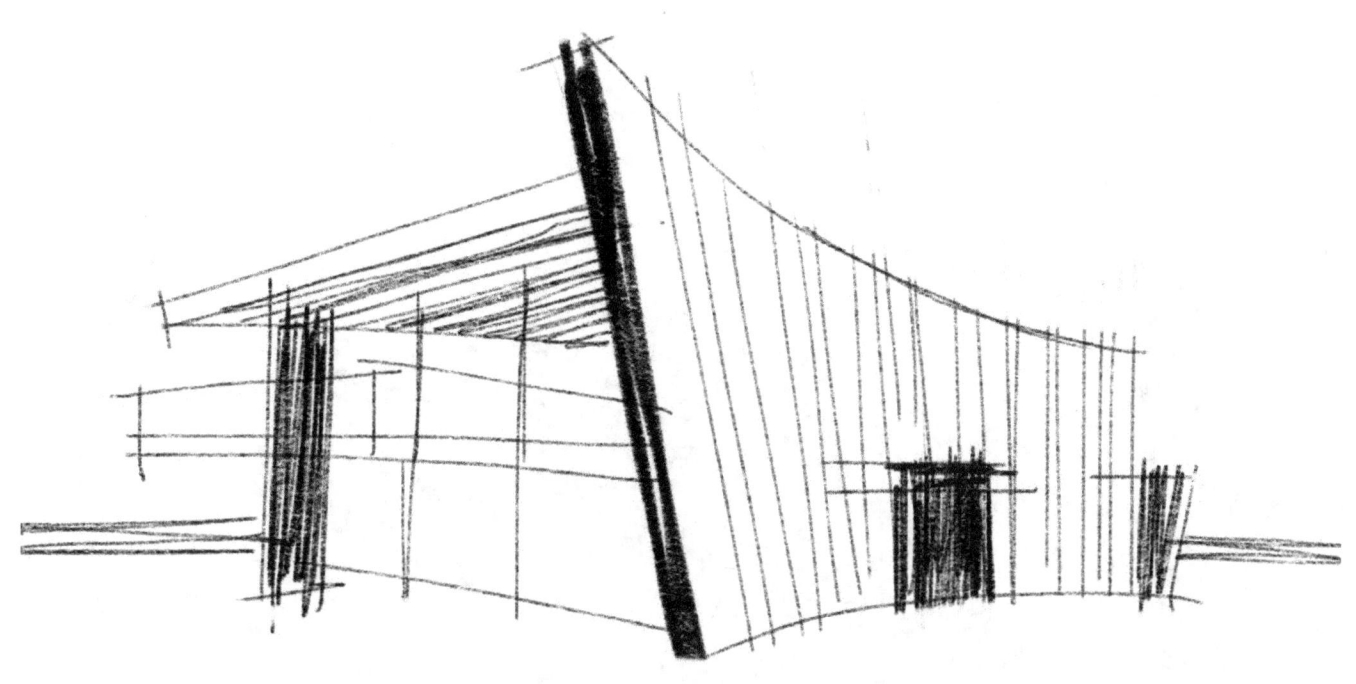

mmmm

About the Author

Ron Lokkesmoe has been involved in many building projects throughout his life, and has a special gift for making unique designs come alive on paper and on the computer. He can also build a home from the bottom up, and designed and built many of his own homes in the magnificent Rocky Mountains.

Being immersed in such spectacular natural beauty, Ron has a deep love and appreciation for nature. That is why his unique designs have always been respectful of their natural surroundings, and why he appreciates the latest designs with green and sustainable components.

Ron studied Art and Design in college, and continues to keep up with the latest trends and techniques in artistic endeavors. From this sketchbook of unique housing designs to an animation project for a corporate client, Ron has the expertise to use many artistic mediums for his creativity.

To bring your visions to life, Ron is available for a free consultation.

RonLokk@gmail.com